HASTINGS

THEN AND NOW

Ken Brooks

By the same author:
Geology and fossils of the Hastings Area

First published in 2002 by S.B. Publications
19 Grove Road, Seaford, East Sussex BN25 1TP
Tel: 01323 893498

ISBN: 1-85770-263-8

Typeset by D. Williams
Printed by Tansleys Printers, 19 Broad Street, Seaford, East Sussex. Tel: (01323) 891019

Front cover: Hastings town centre 1902 and 2002
Back cover: The Old Town beach 1890 - 1900

CONTENTS

ACKNOWLEDGEMENTS, DEDICATION iv

INTRODUCTION v

A BRIEF HISTORY vi

LOCATION MAP 1

THE OLD TOWN 2

THE SEA-FRONT 38

TOWN CENTRE and QUEENS ROAD 58

MOMENTS IN TIME 78

BIBLIOGRAPHY 96

INFORMATION SOURCES 97

INDEX 98

ACKNOWLEDGEMENTS

I should like to thank Dennis Collins, David Padgham, Steve Peak, Brion Purdey, Anne Scott and Cathy Walling for their very helpful advice and information in the preparation of this book. My thanks also go to Phil Cronk, Ray Gladwish, Jean Harvey, Nic Mucci, Richard Pollard, John Vallender, Hastings Museum and Hastings Reference Library for allowing me to use their photographs and illustrations. The wide-angle lens used for some of the photographs was kindly lent by Marriott's Photo Stores. Finally, I am particularly grateful to Diana Williams, without whose love, encouragement and computer skills this book would not have been written.

DEDICATION

This book is dedicated to my parents, Anne and Ivor, and to my sister Christine.

INTRODUCTION

As a local schoolteacher many years ago I believed that the children in my class might gain more pride in their town if they learned something of its past. When Hastings Museum allowed me to make copies of archive prints and photographs for a class topic it was the beginning of my interest in local history.

This book illustrates a nostalgic walk through the Old Town, along the sea-front and into the town centre. Selected photographs and prints from the 19th and early 20th centuries are featured, with the same views taken recently on the opposite page. These often show the enormous changes that have taken place over the years and yet, at the same time, it is interesting to see just how little certain buildings have altered. By making direct comparisons between 'then' and 'now' views we can appreciate what has survived and, in some cases, regret what has been lost.

Around a hundred years ago the photographer was able to set up his tripod and glass-plate camera in the middle of the road or on a purpose-built platform. Attempting to achieve the same viewpoint for this book has occasionally involved avoiding fast-moving traffic or standing on the narrow ledge of a tall building.

With its continuing programme of redevelopment, Hastings is a town which is constantly changing. Because of this, one disadvantage of producing a book which features present-day photographs is that they may be out-of-date soon after the work is published.

In the last section of the book we look at 'Moments in Time', where people and everyday events recorded by the camera provide us with a fascinating glimpse into some of the fashions, pastimes and social attitudes of a bygone age.

A BRIEF HISTORY

The origins of Hastings date back to the Dark Ages, when groups of Jutes and Saxons migrated from mainland Europe and established settlements in the Sussex area. Among these settlers was a tribe known as the Hæstingas, who gave their name to our town. When Duke William of Normandy arrived here in October, 1066, he erected a wooden fort as a base while his troops prepared for the now famous battle.

The present-day town centre was once the site of a natural harbour which gave Hastings important status as one of the Cinque Ports in medieval times. However, from the beginning of the 13th century the harbour gradually became blocked with silt and shingle. This was the worst disaster that could befall a thriving port, and Hastings began to decline when merchants transferred their trade to other towns, such as Winchelsea and Rye.

Attempts were made to build a stone harbour during the reign of Elizabeth I, but the foundations were destroyed by the sea in terrible storms. The last harbour project began in 1896, but this also failed when structural problems and rising costs exhausted all the available funds. Today a fractured sea-wall is all that remains of what might have become a magnificent harbour.

It was during the 18th century, when doctors were promoting the health-giving and curative properties of sea-water, that Hastings began to gain popularity as a seaside 'watering-place'.

When James Barry published his 'Guide to Hastings' in 1797, he claimed that: 'Vice has not yet erected her standard here; the numerous tribe of professional gamblers and swindlers find employment elsewhere. Innocent recreational delight, card assemblies, riding, walking, fishing and other modes of pastime banish care from the mind, whilst the salubrity of the atmosphere impels disease from the body. The society of Hastings enjoy life without mingling in its debaucheries. No watering-place can excel Hastings in the convenience of bathing, and few can equal it'.

Unfortunately, while the holiday trade with its amusements and attractions flourished, the local fishing industry was almost squeezed out of existence.

The development of the sea-front really began in 1835 with the removal of a large outcrop of sandstone, known as the White Rock, for the construction of a promenade road linking Hastings and St. Leonards. The road was later described in the Hastings handbook of 1893: 'The principal parade . . . is paved with cement and lighted by electric lamps. The parade throughout its extent forms an excellent promenade and drive for bath chairs.'

In the 1930s the Borough Engineer, Sidney Little, was responsible for many ambitious projects, including an Olympic-sized Bathing Pool, the first underground car parks in Europe and the reconstruction of the sea-front. His schemes involved the use of huge amounts of cement and, because of this, he was known locally as the 'Concrete King'.

However, it is a very sad fact that 'progressive' redevelopment in Hastings has sometimes involved the demolition of historic buildings. This has been described as 'architectural vandalism' by those who wish to preserve our heritage.

Despite social problems and a gradual decline in recent years, there is now encouraging evidence that Hastings is regaining its position as one of the premier coastal towns in Britain.

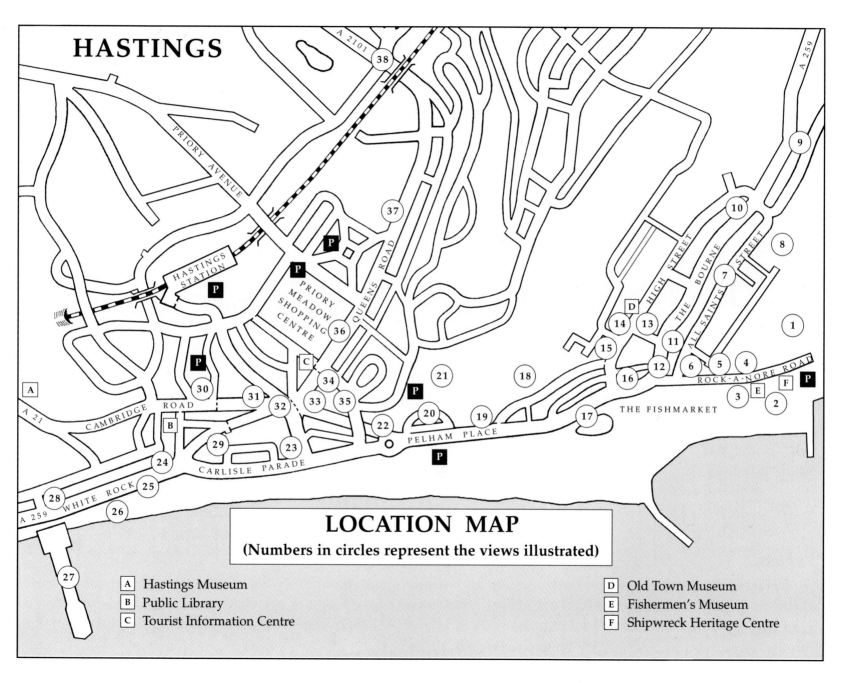

HASTINGS

LOCATION MAP
(Numbers in circles represent the views illustrated)

A Hastings Museum
B Public Library
C Tourist Information Centre

D Old Town Museum
E Fishermen's Museum
F Shipwreck Heritage Centre

PRIORY MEADOW SHOPPING CENTRE

HASTINGS STATION

THE FISHMARKET

PELHAM PLACE

CARLISLE PARADE

WHITE ROCK

CAMBRIDGE ROAD

QUEENS ROAD

PRIORY AVENUE

HIGH STREET

ALL SAINTS STREET

THE BOURNE

ROCK-A-NORE ROAD

A 2101

A 259

A 21

1

VIEW FROM THE EAST HILL   c. 1810

This view of the Old Town shows fishing boats on the beach at the mouth of the Bourne Valley. In the days when road transport was difficult and expensive, large sailing vessels brought in goods such as coal, timber and slate. By beaching at high tide, these boats could then be unloaded into carts when the tide went out. The remains of a 16th century attempt to build a harbour can be seen near the sailing boat on the left.

Hastings Pier marks the sea-front boundary between Hastings and St. Leonards (in the distance). The ruins of Hastings Castle on the West Hill (top right) overlook the town centre and the Old Town. Most of the low-lying area would have been covered by sea at high tide until the 1880s, when a new, large groyne at Rock-a-Nore caused a gradual build-up of shingle on its western side.

THE NET SHOPS   c. 1900

For centuries these tall, wooden sheds have been used by local fishermen for storing their fishing-nets, ropes and sails. With so little space between the cliff and the sea, the local authorities would only rent out small plots of land. However, the fishermen overcame the problem by building their equipment sheds upwards. The name 'net shops' originates from a time when they were used as workshops as well as storage sheds.

The net shops are covered with traditional 'clinker' weather-boarding and most of them measure about 25 feet in height by 8 feet square. Unfortunately, during the past 150 years, many net shops have been destroyed by stormy seas, and in the 1950s some of them were demolished by the Hastings Council as part of a clearance scheme for development of the beach. Luckily, about 45 of these unique structures still survive and are regularly maintained.

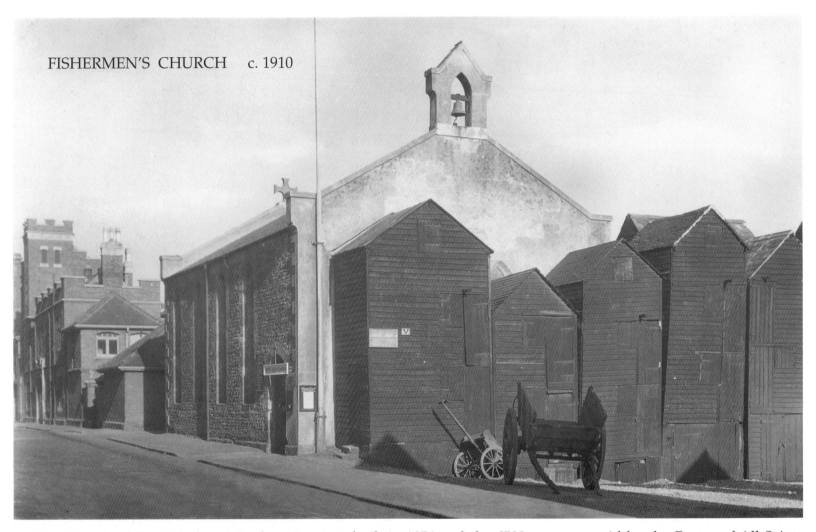

FISHERMEN'S CHURCH   c. 1910

The Church of St. Nicholas at Rock-a-Nore was built in 1854 and the £500 cost was paid by the Rector of All Saints Church from his own pocket. As a Chapel of Ease, it was intended to serve the local fishermen and their families. Its first preacher was Tom Tanner, a missionary who was affectionately known as the 'Reverend Tom', and in 1857 the author, Charles Kingsley, delivered a sermon there. The interior of the building was decorated with shrimp-nets, life-buoys and painted views of the sea.

The church closed in 1939 and during the Second World War it was used as a military store, but by the early 1950s the building had been badly damaged. Fortunately, it was saved from demolition by the Old Hastings Preservation Society and, after restoration, it opened as the Fishermen's Museum in 1956. Its largest and most impressive exhibit is the fishing boat *'Enterprise'*, the last surviving sailing lugger constructed in Hastings. The church font stands in its original position and is still used to baptise the children of local fishermen.

THE TAN HOUSE   c. 1890

In the days before synthetic fibres the 'tan house' in Rock-a-Nore Road used to carry out an important service for local fishermen. For a small fee, their fishing-nets, ropes, sails and clothing would be soaked in a tank of spring water to remove the salt, and then boiled in a cauldron of preservative tanning fluid. This process, known as 'barking', would stain everything to a distinctive brown colour, including their canvas smocks, and it explains why Hastings fishermen were once nicknamed 'tanfrocks'. On the left a large pile of fishing gear is prepared for soaking.

For some time in the 1930s there was a 'swing-out' petrol pump to the right of the building. Its use as a tan house came to an end in 1939 when the road was closed for military reasons during the Second World War. In 1946 the building became the Rock-a-Nore Garage and since 1986 the business has been owned by Nic Mucci.

There was a natural spring in Rock-a-Nore called the East Well which, according to an 1815 guide book, was 'much esteemed as very fine water'. In 1846 about twenty net shops were destroyed in a disastrous fire, but after successful fund-raising efforts by local people, each one was replaced. The remaining cash was used to build this drinking well on the site of the spring. The large poles on the left belonged to Kents, a local boat-building company.

With the slogan 'Waste Not, Want Not' carved on a Portland stone plaque, the East Well still survives as a reminder of the days before piped water. In the 1970s, when the original plaque had become badly worn by erosion, it was replaced by an identical copy. The lower entrance to the East Hill Lift may be seen between the East Well and the Rock-a-Nore Garage, with the 'ice factory' on the right.

EAST CLIFF HOUSE   c. 1965

At the lower end of All Saints Street stands East Cliff House. It was designed and built between 1760 and 1762 by Edward Capell, the Shakespearean critic and official censor of plays, at a cost of £5,000. The house was constructed on the site of the old East Fort, with a gun platform that may have been adapted to form the front terrace of the building. Unfortunately, the house was abandoned during the Second World War and, from then on, it deteriorated rapidly.

After 1950 East Cliff House was used as a fish and chip shop and then as a Bingo hall. In the early 1970s it became the Hastings Arts Workshop until it was eventually converted into Capel's Restaurant. Extensive restoration work has been carried out on the building since 1980. Overlooking the house is the 'castle' structure of the East Hill Lift, a cliff railway which was built in 1902 and is claimed to be the steepest in Britain (1 in 2.8).

ALL SAINTS STREET   c. 1900

Once known as 'Fish Street', its name was changed to All Saints Street when the Hastings Council decided that this would sound more attractive to holiday visitors. The geology of the Bourne Valley is reflected by the raised pavement on the eastern side (left), where tightly-packed houses are built into the hillside. In fact, in medieval times most of Hastings was contained in this narrow valley between the East and West Hills.

The medieval house in the centre with an overhanging upper floor is one of the oldest buildings in Hastings. According to a local story, it was once owned by the mother of a famous 17th century admiral, Sir Cloudesley Shovell. In recent times a few guests at the house claim to have seen the ghost of a lady in black. Several houses in All Saints Street still have 'priest holes', secret passages and connected lofts through which smugglers would escape.

ALL SAINTS CHURCH   c. 1820

When the earliest All Saints Church was damaged by the sea it was rebuilt further inland, but this building was destroyed during a raid by the French in the Hundred Years War. The present All Saints Church, which dates from the early 15th century, has a small pyramidal peak, called a Sussex Cap, on its tower. In the 18th century a church warden used to wake those who snored during services, while an official 'dog-whipper' would chase dogs out of the church.

During restoration work in 1870, a medieval mural was discovered on the wall above the chancel arch. It is known as the 'Doom' painting as it depicts the Last Judgement, with the Devil hanging 'the damned' on gallows instead of casting them into hell-fire. The old churchyard contains a number of interesting graves, including the headstone of a local fisherman, Joseph Swaine, who was shot and killed in 1821 during a search of his boat by a customs officer.

THE MARKET CROSS   c. 1910

The Market Cross stood at the junction of Old London Road and Harold Road, but despite its local name, there is no record of a market at this site in early documents. In fact, the stone cross was erected to commemorate the accession of Edward VII in 1901. A tram stands at the end of its rails, as this was as close as they were allowed to the Old Town. Despite much opposition to their arrival in 1905, the trams became very popular and provided Hastings with an efficient transport system for many years.

Before St. Leonards was built in the 19th century, Old London Road (left) was the main route into Hastings. When the new Bourne road was carved through the Old Town in the 1950s, much of this area was redesigned. During road-widening and landscaping alterations, the Market Cross was moved southwards into a shrub garden between Old London Road and Harold Road.

THE OLD STABLES   c. 1950

These stables were built at the top of High Street between 1739 and 1746 for Old Hastings House, the nearby home of John Collier. He was a wealthy and influential town clerk who helped to transform Hastings from a poor fishing village into a fashionable seaside holiday resort. At the end of the 18th century, when Britain was threatened with a French invasion, the stables were converted into barracks for the Duke of Wellington's troops.

By the mid-1950s, the abandoned stables were in a very poor condition, but luckily they were saved from demolition by the Old Hastings Preservation Society. After much interior reconstruction, the building was opened as the Stables Theatre by Sir Ralph Richardson in June 1959. Extensions to the Theatre were added by the Stables Trust in 1977 and 2000.

THE BOURNE THEATRE   c. 1930

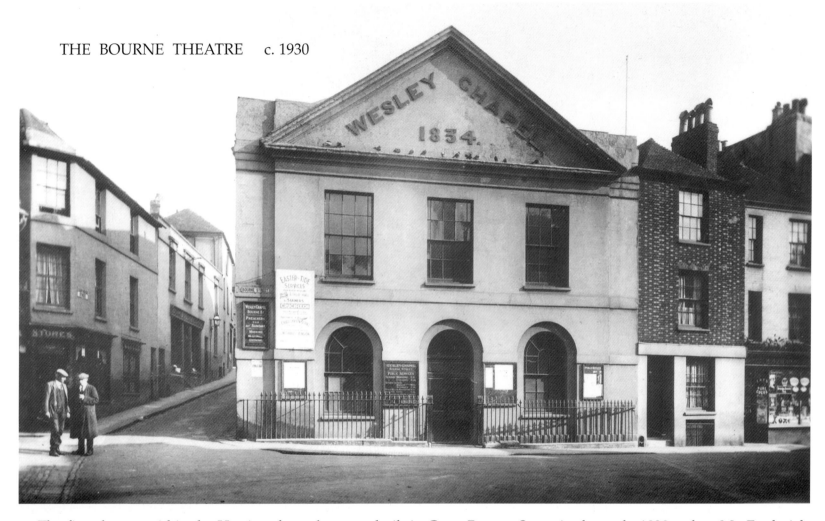

The first theatre within the Hastings boundary was built in Great Bourne Street in the early 1820s when Mr. Frederick Brooke was finally granted a licence by the local authorities. This was a time when actors were classed as 'rogues and vagabonds' and local authorities believed that this form of entertainment 'demoralised the lower classes of society'. The Bourne Theatre opened with a production of *As You Like It* on 18th August 1825, but despite the enthusiastic efforts of its manager and company, the theatre closed after only eight years, mainly through a lack of support.

In 1833 the abandoned theatre was bought by local Wesleyans who promptly burned the scenery and converted it into a chapel. The building was partly demolished in 1940 and replaced by a Neo-Georgian style structure. In the 1950s the front of the chapel was rebuilt during construction work on The Bourne, a new main road through the Old Town. The hall was sold by the Wesleyans in the 1970s and it is presently used as an Arts Centre and a venue for exhibitions.

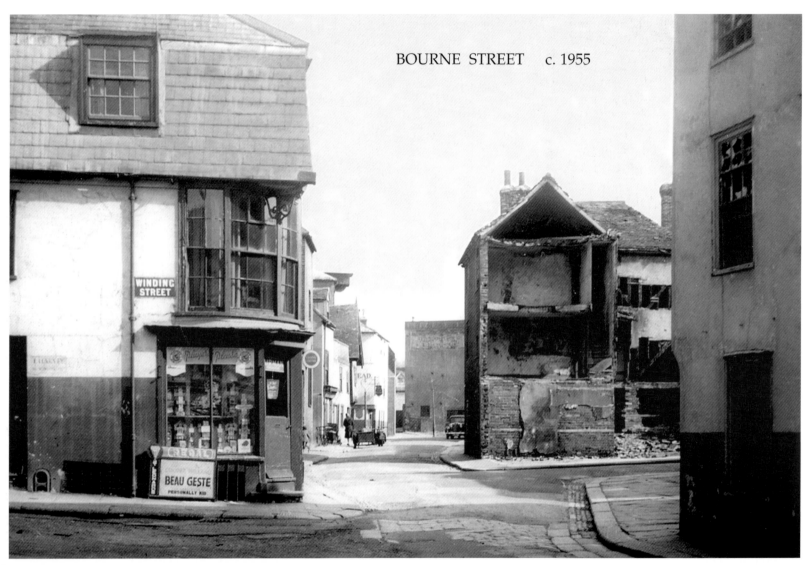

BOURNE STREET   c. 1955

This road follows the ancient course of the Bourne, a stream which gave its name to the Old Town valley. After flowing down from Ore, the Bourne Stream was contained in a large pond near the junction of High Street and All Saints Street. During the 18th century, sluice gates were opened when the pond was full so that water would flow through the streets, allowing residents to fill their jugs before rubbish and sewage were washed into the sea.

By 1832 the Bourne Stream had become so polluted that its water supply was diverted into a reservoir higher up the valley. The stream's channel was paved over and the pond was filled in, later to form the garden of a house called 'The Wilderness'. During the 1950s a number of Old Town buildings were demolished to make way for The Bourne, which was eventually completed in 1960.

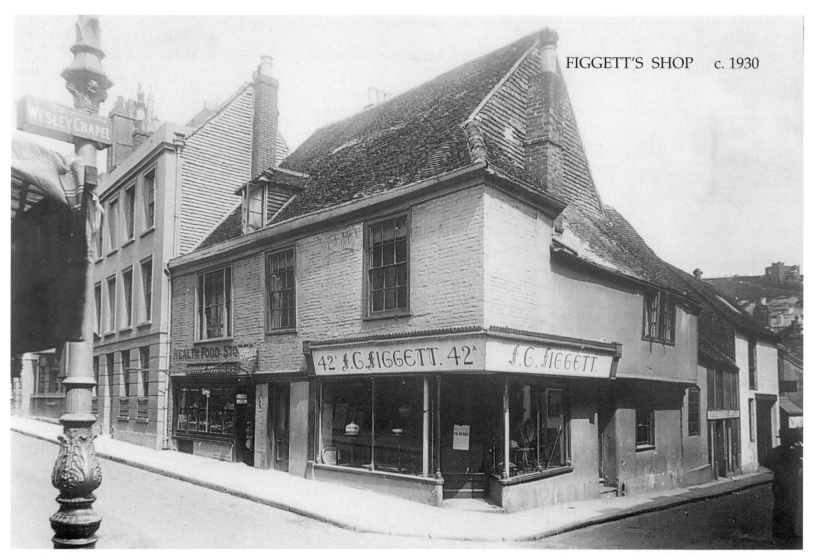

FIGGETT'S SHOP   c. 1930

This building at the corner of High Street and Courthouse Street dates from around 1500. From the mid-1920s it was an antique shop owned by Mr. Figgett, but when Reeves' Furniture Warehouse on the opposite corner was bombed in 1943, Figgett's was badly damaged by the blast. It is interesting to see that a Health Food Store occupied part of the building in the 1930s. The top 'station' of the East Hill Lift may be seen on the right-hand side of the picture.

After 1968 the shop was owned by Mr. H. Lucy, a violin restorer, until it was bought by the Binns family in 1974. Today, as Stone Corner, it is the only shop in Hastings which specialises in minerals and fossils. During recent restoration work what may prove to be a 16th century window with its original glass and a number of surrounding beams were discovered under the plaster of an outside wall. These may be seen on the Courthouse Street side of the building.

OLD TOWN HALL   c. 1825

The first Hastings Town Hall and Magistrates Court was constructed here in 1700. It included an open market-place on the ground floor and, in fact, High Street was known as Market Street until the early 19th century. This 1820s painting shows the Town Hall after it was rebuilt in a style very similar to its original design. In 1881 it was abandoned when civic services were moved to the present Town Hall in Queens Road.

After 1881 the old Town Hall building was used as a police station, offices and then as a furniture store. Windows were built into the arches in 1949 when the ground floor became the Old Town Museum of Local History, and a branch of the Public Library opened on the first floor. As its collections increased, the Museum eventually took over the whole building. The exhibits and displays have recently been redesigned and 'modernised'.

THE SWAN HOTEL   c. 1880

In the 18th century the Swan Hotel was the centre of social life in the Old Town, with grand dinners and assemblies held in large rooms. It was also the main terminus for stage-coaches travelling to and from London, Brighton and Dover. An archway from the High Street led through to a large courtyard with extensive stabling - and there was even a brewery! The hotel was demolished in 1889 and rebuilt on the same site, but on a smaller scale.

The new Swan Hotel survived until the Second World War. Then, in May 1943, it was destroyed during a bombing raid and, tragically, many lives were lost. Some years after the War a block of retirement flats, Swan House, was built on the site with an open space set aside as a memorial garden.

THE 'ROTUNDA' FISHMARKET   c. 1890

The seaward end of the High Street has always been a traditional site for fish selling in the Old Town. This 'rotunda' for retail fishmongers was built here by the Hastings Corporation in 1870 and remained in use until the 1920s. When luggers returned with their catches of fish they would be sold locally or transported to markets in other towns. The fish were packed in wooden boxes with ice which was manufactured at an 'ice house' in Rock-a-Nore Road.

The rotunda structure was demolished in 1928 to provide the trolley-buses with a turning circle, which remained in use until the 'trolleys' were replaced by motor buses in 1959. With limited space for cars in the Old Town, the site has since been used as a parking area. Remains of the medieval town wall may be seen behind the flats in the background.

The Lifeboat House was erected on Marine Parade by a London builder in 1882. It was paid for from the legacy of Charles Arcoll, a former mayor of Maidstone and wholesale greengrocer, who was born in Hastings. He left £2,000 for the purchase of a lifeboat, its carriage and a boathouse. In stormy conditions the lifeboat often had to be pulled some distance along the sea-front by horses to find a safe launching site. Note the lines of washing tied across the beach.

The boating lake was constructed here in 1933 on a gradually increasing beach area. When a new Lifeboat House was built on the Stade in 1949 the original building remained beside the boating lake as a landmark. It was used as a venue by the Sea-Scouts until 1959 when the structure was demolished to widen the sea-front road through the Old Town. The present Lifeboat House was opened in the 1980s to contain the *'Sealink Endeavour'*.

THE 'HARBOUR ARM'   c. 1900

Work began in 1896 on the construction of a harbour with two concrete walls or 'arms' extending from the Old Town beach. Steady progress was made until the end of 1897, when an ancient river channel in the bedrock was discovered in the path of the western arm. The costs incurred by extra materials and delays increased dramatically until the Harbour Company was declared bankrupt and building work came to an end. The wooden gantry (left) was designed to allow the eastward drift of shingle through to the Rock-a-Nore groyne.

This view shows all that remains of the harbour's western 'arm'. Although the wooden gantry did not last for very long, the build-up of shingle against the Rock-a-Nore groyne and the harbour wall since 1900 has made a 'contribution' to the Old Town. It has greatly extended the fishermen's beach and provided more space for boats, storage sheds and a fish market. At the same time, a boating lake and other amusements have appeared!

This building opened as a music hall theatre on Easter Saturday 1899, with Marie Lloyd topping the bill. Two years later it was renamed the Marine Theatre of Varieties. One of the theatre's special features was its cantilevered balcony which had no pillars to block views of the stage. By 1910, moving pictures had become a more popular attraction and the theatre was converted into the Royal Cinema De Luxe.

In 1965 the De Luxe closed as a cinema with *'She'*, starring Ursula Andress, as its final film. Sadly, much of the original interior structure was removed or rebuilt before it reopened as the De Luxe Bingo Club and Amusement Centre in 1970, although the exterior, with its marvellous façade of terracotta tiles, has survived. For many years this building has been affectionately known as 'the De Loo'.

Pelham Crescent, with the Church of St-Mary-in-the-Castle as its centre-piece, was designed by Joseph Kay and built between 1824 and 1828. The Crescent has been described as 'one of the finest Regency compositions on the south coast'. The church has many unusual features including a huge, domed roof and a circular auditorium with seating for over 500. There is also a natural spring and an immersion font as well as catacombs which were last used for a burial in 1854.

With falling attendances, the church was declared redundant by the Church of England and closed in 1970. By 1987 the abandoned building was derelict and demolition seemed certain. Fortunately, the roof was repaired by Hastings Borough Council and English Heritage and through fund-raising efforts by the Friends of St. Mary-in-the-Castle, the building has been beautifully restored. It was converted into an Arts Centre and opened to the public in 1997.

HASTINGS CASTLE   c. 1830

The West Hill is the traditional site of a wooden fortress which was hastily erected by William the Conqueror in October 1066. After the Norman Conquest the structure was replaced by a more permanent stone castle. Although known as Hastings 'Castle', these ruins are, in fact, the remains of the Collegiate Church of St. Mary within the castle grounds. Thomas à Becket was the Dean of this church for a short time and, although there is no record that he ever came to Hastings, it is claimed that his ghost haunts the castle.

By the end of the 18th century the castle had long been abandoned and was in ruins. Between 1815 and 1820 a large part of the site, known as the Gun Garden, was removed to build Pelham Crescent and St. Mary-in-the-Castle Church below the cliff (left). The castle was owned by the Earl of Chichester and the Pelham family before it was purchased for £3,000 by the Hastings Corporation in 1951 and opened to the public.

CASTLE STREET   c. 1900

Mastin Brothers opened their drapery store (on the right) in 1872 and, as their business expanded, they gradually took over all the premises from numbers 7 to 12 Castle Street. After surviving a disastrous fire in 1904, the store front was redesigned and 'modernised'. Further improvements in 1931 were reported by the Hastings Observer: 'A covered canopy, 100 feet in length, enables shoppers to view their attractive window display at leisure on rainy days'. During the 1950s and 1960s the building on the left was occupied by Abraham's, a radio and television shop.

22

After Abraham's moved to Queens Road, in the early 1960s, the building was demolished and an Italian restaurant was later built on the site. Mastin's remained a very popular family business until its closure in 1969. The store then stood empty until 1972 (its centenary year) when it was sold for demolition and redevelopment. It was replaced by a modern glass and concrete structure with the frozen food store, Iceland, on the ground floor and offices above.

THE QUEEN'S HOTEL   c. 1900

Eight houses were originally planned for this site on the south-west corner of Harold Place. Instead, after construction work lasting nearly four years and at a cost of £27,000, the Queens Hotel opened here in 1864. A report in the local newspaper declared: 'The Hotel will, we trust, be well appreciated by its aristocratic visitors'. The building was designed with a classical style entrance in Harold Place and a forecourt that marked the end of the sea-front road from St. Leonards.

23

During the early 1930s the promenade was extended across the front of the hotel to join up with the Old Town 'parade' at Denmark Place. The main entrance was re-sited to face the sea and the two 'cupola' towers were removed when they became unsafe. By the end of the 1980s the Queens Hotel was in a very poor condition, but with exterior repainting in 2001, it once again became one of the most impressive buildings on the sea-front.

White and Norton, the drapers, was originally the premises of the famous coach-building company James Rock and Son. In 1835 one of their carriages, the Royal Victoria, was claimed to be a 'revelation in the possibilities of coach travelling'. When the White Rock Brewery and the Seaside and Pier Hotel were demolished in 1885, one of Britain's first 'skyscrapers', the Palace Hotel, was built on the site.

24

The Palace Hotel is now occupied by International House, an English language school, while Courts the furniture shop has replaced White and Norton's. In 1910 Fred Judges' Photo Store was taken over by Mr. Marriott who later became a director of the company. In June 2002 a blue plaque commemorating 100 years since Judges started, was placed by the entrance to Marriott's Photo Stores.

WHITE ROCK BATHS c. 1890

An ambitious private scheme to construct public baths under the parade began in 1874. The work involved extending the parade, then only ten feet wide, to form the roof of the building. Near the centre of the picture are the separate entrances to the Ladies' and Gentlemen's Swimming Baths. The main swimming bath was 165 feet (50 metres) in length, and for many years it was the largest covered bath in Britain. Films were shown as an extra attraction in the early 1900s.

25

The White Rock Baths were purchased by the Hastings Corporation in 1925 and, during the next five years, £100,000 was spent on reconstruction work. By 1937 they offered Turkish, slipper and medicinal baths, while the seaweed baths were especially popular. However, unable to compete with the larger and more modern bath which opened at the Hastings Sports Centre in the 1970s, the building was converted into an ice-skating rink for a few years.

BATHING MACHINES   c. 1890

The bathing machines in front of Carlisle Parade were blue and white striped sheds on high iron wheels with steps at the back and front. Horses were used to pull these mobile changing rooms to the water's edge and then back up the beach as the tide came in. The earlier bathing machines had large canvas hoods which extended down to the water-level for bathing in complete privacy. Before 1903 men and women had to keep at least 100 yards apart in the water.

26

After 1906 the heavy bathing machines were gradually replaced by canvas cabins until, eventually, only a towel was required for changing on the beach. The picture shows where, in 1928-31, the road and promenade between White Rock Place and the Queens Hotel were extended by seventy feet towards the sea. This project also included the first underground car park to be built in Europe.

HASTINGS PIER   c. 1910

Hastings Pier was opened on 5th August 1872, in pouring rain on the first official Bank Holiday! The ceremony was performed by Earl Granville, Lord Warden of the Cinque Ports, and Thomas Brassey, a generous benefactor to the town The entire length of the Pier was over 900 feet from the promenade, with continuous lines of cast-iron seating along its sides. At the far end was a magnificent pavilion, built in the Moorish style, containing a large theatre with seating for over 700 people. Apart from the pavilion there were no other buildings on the Pier until 1908.

27

In 1914 the shore end of the Pier was bought by the Hastings Corporation as part of a sea-front improvements scheme. This section, known as the 'parade extension', was widened to build a circular bandstand surrounded by shelters and kiosks. Sadly, the pavilion and its theatre were destroyed by a spectacular fire in July 1917. The theatre was rebuilt in the 1920s and since 2001 the Pier has been redesigned and modernised as a private venture.

THE EAST SUSSEX HOSPITAL   c. 1900

The East Sussex Hospital, built in 1886/87, was an impressive structure with wards in its two end 'towers'. The curved walls were believed to allow better air circulation and prevent germs from lurking in corners. Patients could often be seen 'taking the sea air' on open balconies overlooking Hastings Pier. Eventually the building was demolished when a new East Sussex Hospital opened in Cambridge Road in 1923.

28

The original East Sussex Hospital was replaced by the White Rock Pavilion, a beautifully designed theatre which was officially opened in April 1927 by Edward, Prince of Wales. It was built for the Hastings Municipal Orchestra and soon became a very popular venue for concerts and summer shows such as the 'Fol-de-Rols' and 'Twinkle'. The Pavilion was refurbished during the 1980s and renamed the White Rock Theatre.

THE AMERICA GROUND   c. 1845

This was the site of the Saxon harbour which, by the 15th century, had become blocked with shingle and silt. By 1800 the area was settled on by rope-makers, merchants and squatters living in shacks and abandoned boat hulks. When they hoisted an American flag to show their independence from the Hastings authorities, this 'no-man's-land' became known as the 'America Ground'. To the left is the Coastguard Station on Cuckoo Hill, with the Priory Meadows beyond.

29

After a public enquiry in 1827 to establish ownership of the America Ground, it was decided that the land belonged to the Crown. The inhabitants were offered seven-year leases and in 1835 the area was cleared for development. In 1849 Patrick F. Robertson, a wealthy London merchant, leased the land from the Crown to begin his building projects on the site. These included Robertson Street and Trinity Street which were completed by 1855.

The Holy Trinity Priory was founded on this site around 1175 by the Augustinian Order known as the Black Canons. From at least the early 18th century the land was occupied by the Priory Farm until building development began in 1872. When the Ritz Cinema opened here in 1938, it soon became very popular as a high-class venue for entertainment. Among its attractions were live performances on the stage and 'ABC Minors' Saturday morning film shows for children.

30

The Ritz Cinema was later known as the ABC Cinema, but unfortunately it closed rather abruptly in 1971 when the site was sold for development. The demolition of the building provided archaeologists with a brief opportunity to examine the site of the ancient Priory. Soon construction work began on a Sainsbury's supermarket which opened in 1974, but a few years later the premises were taken over by the Co-op and then by the retail store ESK.

THE PUBLIC HALL   c. 1910

The Public Hall in the town centre was originally built as a 'music hall' in the 1850s. It was here, on 6th November 1861, that Charles Dickens read extracts from his *'Christmas Carol'* and *'Pickwick Papers'*. The building was converted into the Public Hall in 1875, and was used for meetings and various forms of entertainment. Later, during the early 1900s, magic lantern shows became a very popular attraction here.

In July 1913 the Public Hall opened as a cinema and in 1930 it was 'modernised' to become the Plaza Cinema. After the Second World War it was renamed the Orion Cinema, with W. H. Smith occupying the ground floor. When the cinema closed in 1978 its last film was *'Star Wars'*. A year later the whole building was taken over by Smiths and then later by Yates's Wine Lodges.

When Prince Albert died in 1861, the Hastings Council agreed that a clock tower should be erected at the town centre in his memory. After a national competition to find a suitable design it was built of Portland stone in 1863, complete with a life-size statue of Albert. The 'Memorial' clock tower soon became a popular landmark and meeting place for local people. The Post Office (left) was at this site in Queens Road from 1868 until 1930.

Sadly, when the Memorial tower was damaged by a mysterious fire in April 1973, the Hastings Council voted for its demolition. All that remains is the statue of Prince Albert which was taken to a greenhouse in Alexandra Park. In the early 1990s the town centre became a pedestrian precinct, with only one road crossing through it. Even today, the site is still referred to as the 'Memorial' by those who remember the clock tower.

MEADOW COTTAGES   c. 1865

MEADOW
ROAD.

MEADOW
COTTAGES

These cottages were built near the town centre in 1823. In 1876 Meadow Road was renamed 'Queens Road' in honour of Queen Victoria and, when Ore became part of the Hastings Borough in 1897, the other Queens Road on the Vine Farm estate in Ore Village became Victoria Avenue.

The General Post Office was built on the site of 1 to 3 Meadow Cottages in 1869. After the G.P.O. moved to its present location in Cambridge Road in 1930, the building was taken over by Wards, the men's outfitters. Since 1995 the shop has been occupied by Halifax plc.

THE GAIETY THEATRE c. 1910

The Gaiety opened as a theatre in Queens Road in August 1882, and it soon became a venue for many famous performers and politicians. These included Harry Houdini, Lillie Langtry and Oscar Wilde, and in 1891 Mr. Gladstone addressed a meeting here. The theatre's varied productions included repertory, musical comedy, pantomime and opera. Its last show was a production of *'The Desert Song'*, performed by the Hastleons, a local theatre group.

In 1932 the theatre was converted into the Gaiety Cinema. Since 1967 it has been renamed the Classic, the Cannon, the ABC and the Odeon. On the right-hand side of the cinema is the entrance to Queens Arcade where John Logie Baird rented an attic above a flower shop for his first television experiments in the early 1920s. The open space in the centre of the picture marks the site of buildings which were demolished for road widening in the 1990s.

THE CASTLE HOTEL   c. 1900

The Castle Hotel was built in the Regency style on the site of a thatched cottage which had a reputation as a 'gin house'. After the hotel opened in 1817, Wellington Square was completed around an oval-shaped, private garden (right) for residents. In fact, this building project was the first important stage in the development of the Priory Valley and the present-day town centre. For many years the lower part of the square was used as a terminus for country buses.

The Castle Hotel had a large dance floor, where Phyllis Godfrey gave dancing lessons in the early 1960s. The bar was well-known locally for its beer pumps labelled: 'Boys' (mild), 'Growing Boys' (bitter) and 'Old Boys' (strong bitter - Worthington E). Sadly, the hotel was demolished in 1966 to build a Tesco supermarket which later became an indoor market and then a 'Pound-Stretcher' store.

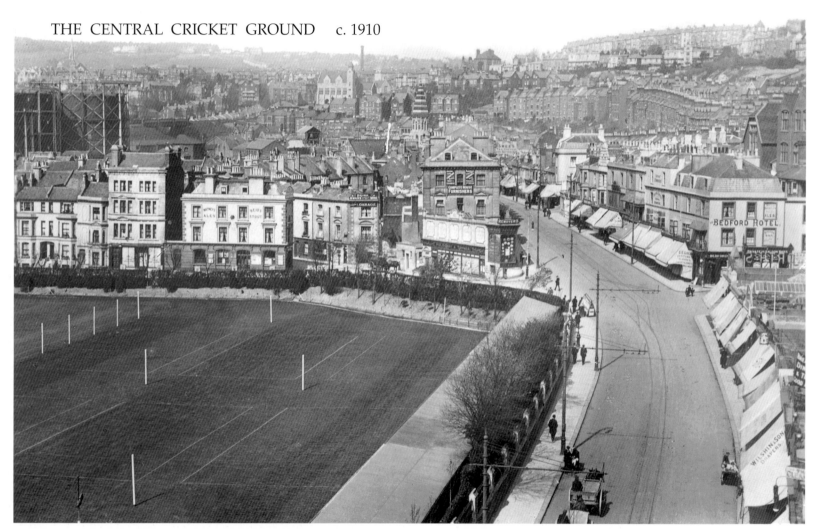

THE CENTRAL CRICKET GROUND   c. 1910

In Saxon and Norman times the area which now extends from the town centre to this part of Queens Road was the inner part of a natural harbour. This later became marshland until it was drained for building development in the 1830s. Part of the site, by then known as the Priory Meadows, was left open for a Central Cricket and Recreation Ground. The river which once flowed into the harbour is now reduced to a small stream that runs through Alexandra Park and under Queens Road.

72

During 1995 there was much controversy when the Central Cricket Ground was transformed into a huge building site as work began on a complex of modern shops. Two years later the opening of the Priory Meadow Shopping Centre was celebrated with a visit by Her Majesty the Queen. It was here in 1951 that, as Princess Elizabeth, she had received the deeds of Hastings Castle and presented them to the Mayor for safe keeping.

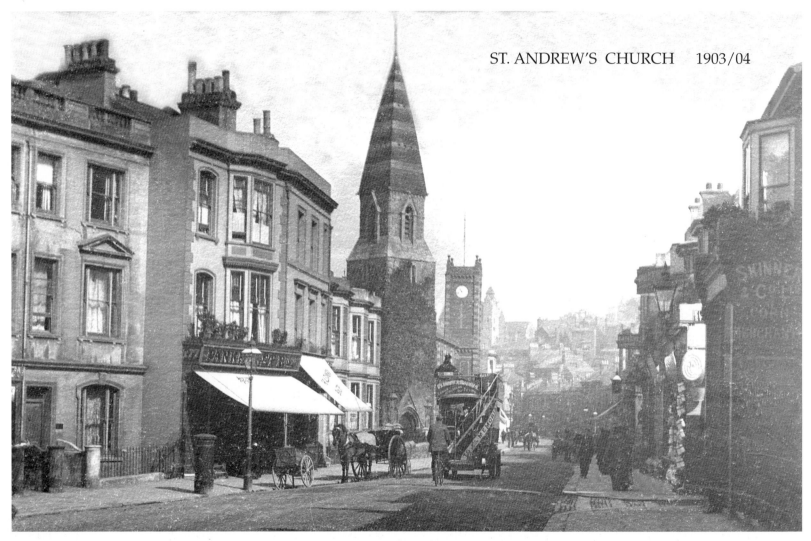

ST. ANDREW'S CHURCH   1903/04

The Church of St. Andrew was built in Queens Road in 1869 and was consecrated the following year by the Bishop of Chichester. The first vicar, George Hodges, was so eloquent in the pulpit that in 1873 the church had to be enlarged to accommodate his increasing congregation. In 1904/5 the walls of the chancel were decorated with murals painted by Robert Tressell, the local author of *'The Ragged Trousered Philanthropists'*. A Milnes Daimler motor-bus is approaching the church and the red-bricked tower of the Gas Board showrooms beyond it.

37

Unfortunately, with falling attendances and parish reorganisation, St. Andrew's Church was closed in 1969 and it soon became derelict. A year later the building was demolished, but not before some of Tressell's damaged murals were rescued and restored for display in the Hastings Museum. The site is now a Safeway's petrol station with their supermarket and car park behind it.

Before Hastings Station opened in 1851, a massive earth embankment was constructed across the Priory Valley for the railway line to Ashford and Rye. A narrow road tunnel, known as St. Andrew's Archway, was built into the embankment at the top of Queens Road (then called Ore Lane). In 1882 it was described by the printer, William Ransom, as 'a dungeon-like railway arch which casts a gloom over one of the prettiest spots in Hastings'.

38

Passengers on the open-top deck of horse omnibuses had to duck their heads to avoid the curved sides of the low tunnel. During the 1890s the height of the railway embankment was increased and a new iron bridge was constructed. This typical Victorian bridge was designed in the classical style with massive, fluted columns. In November 1898 the old St. Andrew's Archway was at last demolished for road widening.

MOMENTS IN TIME

We will now look at a few 'snapshots' from the lives of ordinary people who lived in Hastings when many of the early photographs in this book were taken. From the middle of the 19th century character studies and family portraits were popular subjects for photographers. One of the most outstanding of these was George Woods, a cameraman who recorded many wonderful scenes of everyday life in the 1890s (pages: 79 to 89). Some of the pictures in this section have been printed directly from his original glass negatives.

A fisherman sits in his net shop to check and repair nets known as 'prawn gins' while a trawl hangs down beside him. The open doors reveal how the net shops were used to store a variety of fishing equipment, and the structure is raised on blocks to allow sea-water to pass underneath at high tide. The girl was probably posed in the picture by the photographer.

This fisherman, wearing a sou'-wester hat, stirs a cauldron containing an unknown brew. He may be melting tar for waterproofing his boat or perhaps boiling shrimps or fish scraps for supper. The fishing boat behind him has a concave 'lute' stern so that, when returning to an open beach, breaking waves would be forced under the hull.

Two of these local fishermen are wearing traditional peaked caps and jerseys while the third man wears a bowler hat and smock. This clothing was common among the fishing community during the late 19th and the early 20th century. Beards and clay pipes were also fashionable at this time.

These children drinking fresh spring water from the East Well provided another opportunity for George Woods' natural photography. When the handle was pulled water poured out through a bronze lion's head, and the funnel on the left was probably used for filling bottles.

In the 1890s William Dines' barber's shop was in East Beach Street, near the London Trader public house. Mr. Dine holds a telescope while his son, also called William, enjoys a joke with him. When Mr. Dine spotted a visiting boat with his telescope he would row out to offer haircuts and shaves to the sailors.

In the days before clothes were designed especially for children, most young people had to wear 'handed-down' clothes. This tended to give them the appearance of miniature adults. Apart from one boy who looks at the camera, the children are totally absorbed in their own thoughts.

An ice-cream seller and her friend exchange the latest gossip in 1894. The ice-cream was packed in crushed ice to keep it cold and sold in glasses for one penny or a halfpenny. This sea-front site is Denmark Place, which was later bombed during the Second World War and then demolished.

The goat and trap was a popular novelty with children during the 1890s, but as with other carriages, it required a licence from the Hastings Council. This location is Robertson Terrace, once the main sea-front road which ended at the Queens Hotel. In old postcards one of these goat carts is occasionally seen waiting near the entrance to Hastings Pier.

The 'Bird Lady' in Harold Place at the town centre. For one penny the lady would get her caged bird to pick a card which would tell your fortune. Boats have been pulled up from the beach above the high tide mark and the Albert Memorial clock tower can be seen in the background.

These ladies and girls, all dressed in the latest styles of the 1890s, are standing outside the pavilion on Hastings Pier. The photograph gives the impression that smiling at the camera was strictly forbidden in Victorian times! The two models behind them may be part of an exhibition - perhaps featuring buildings made from matchsticks?

A beach scene in front of the Queens Hotel before an extensive area of sand was later covered by shingle. This was the landing-place for large pleasure-yachts such as the *'Albertine'*, where a wide gap in the promenade also allowed smaller boats to be pulled up into Harold Place (centre).

Despite her undignified appearance, this lady is determined to have her paddle in the sea. For many people, this activity was considered to be obligatory during a trip to the seaside. The absence of the East Hill Lift in the background indicates that this photograph dates from before 1902.

This thresher shark, which had become entangled in a fisherman's net, provided an ideal opportunity for a group photograph in April 1927. The name 'thresher' comes from their method of hunting fish. Using their long tails, these sharks herd small fish or squid into a tight group and stun them with a swipe of the tail.

This drinking fountain stood in front of the 'rotunda' at the lower end of the High Street. The boy is drinking from a cast-iron cup which was used by everyone, as this was a time when people were apparently unaware of the risk of spreading infection.

In 1919 this German submarine, which measured 182 feet (55 m) in length, was allocated to France as war compensation. On 19th April it was on tow to Cherbourg when the cable broke in rough seas, and the following morning local residents were amazed to see the huge submarine washed up on the beach near Harold Place. It remained there long enough for curiosity to be replaced by indifference, until it was eventually cut up for scrap metal.

During 1904/05 nearly all of the main roads in Hastings were in a chaotic condition while the rails were being laid down for the first electric trams in the town. Our present-day road works may seem insignificant when compared with the problems that must have been caused at that time.

This photograph from 1926/27 shows two solid-tyre motor-buses attempting to pass each other in the High Street, a manoeuvre which would be impossible today with the continuous parking along the road. The open-top bus is a Leyland 'Leviathan' with 59 seats.

BIBLIOGRAPHY (in chronological order)

Hastings of Bygone Days and the Present by Henry Cousins. F. J. Parsons, 1911.

Hastings, a Survey of Times Past and Present by Anthony Belt. Kenneth Saville, 1937.

Historic Hastings. 2nd ed. by J. Manwaring Baines. F. J. Parsons, 1963.

Outline of Hastings History. 5th ed. by J. Manwaring Baines. Hastings Museum, 1975.

Hastings: a pictorial history by D. Robert Elleray. Phillimore, 1979. ISBN: 0 85033 324 5.

George Woods: Victorian photographer of Hastings by Irene Rhoden. Hastings Museum and Art Gallery, 1984.

Fishermen of Hastings by Steve Peak. New Books, 1985. ISBN: 0 9510706 0 6.

Old Town Hastings by James Meredith. Meredith Press, 1986. ISBN: 0 9511486 0 5.

George Woods: photographs from the 1890s by Irene Rhoden & Steve Peak. Midnight P., 1987. ISBN: 1 85360 000 8.

Hastings: a living history by David Thornton. Hastings Publishing Co., 1987. ISBN: 0 9512201 0 1.

Hastings in Old Photographs by Pamela Haines. Alan Sutton, 1989. ISBN: 0 86299 621 X.

Hastings in Old Photographs: a second selection by Pamela Haines. Alan Sutton, 1991. ISBN: 0 86299 683 8.

Hastings and the 1066 Country by David Arscott & David Brook. S. B. Publications, 1993. ISBN: 1 85770 049 X.

Hastings Tramways by Robert J. Harley. Middleton Press, 1993. ISBN: 1 873793 18 9.

Hastings in Old Picture Postcards by Anne Scott. European Library, 1993. ISBN: 90 288 5582 3

That's All Folks! (local cinemas) by Nick Prince. Mercia Cinema Society, 1996. ISBN: 0 946406 40 5

Hastings & St. Leonards-on-Sea by Gavin Haines. Sutton Publishing, 1997. ISBN: 0 7509 1355 X.

Priory Meadow and the Town Centre by Hastings Modern History Workshop. HMHW, 1997. ISBN: 0 9529766 1 7.

Hastings Past by Rex Marchant. Phillimore & Co., 1997. ISBN: 1 86077 046 0.

Hastings Bygones by the Hastings Local History Group. 1998. ISSN: 1465 1246.

The Hastings & St. Leonards Omnibus Company 1877 - 1906 by Cliff Mewett. CD Publications, 1998.

Hastings by Tony Wales. (Archive Photographs Series). Chalford, 1998. ISBN: 0 7524 1109 8.

Heroes, Villains and Others from Hastings by Mary Haskell Porter. Ferndale Press, 1999. ISBN: 1 870096 03 7.

The local studies room at Hastings Museum contains most of these books and other research material.

INFORMATION SOURCES

East Sussex Records Office: The Maltings, Castle Precincts, Lewes.   01273 482349

Fishermen's Museum: Rock-a-Nore Road.   Hastings.   01424 461446

Friends of St. Mary-in-the Castle Charitable Trust, Ltd. (F.O.S.M.I.C.):   Hastings.   01424 430580

Hastings & Rother Family History Society: Ore Community Centre, Hastings.   01424 436605

Hastings Area Archaeological Research Group (HAARG):   Hastings.   01424 443752

Hastings Borough Council: Town Hall, Queens Road, Hastings.   01424 781066

Hastings Local History Group: Hastings.   01424 431134

Hastings Museum & Art Gallery: John's Place, Bohemia Road, Hastings.   01424 781155

Hastings Museum of Local History: Old Town Hall, High Street, Hastings.   01424 781166

Hastings Reference Library: Brassey Institute, 13 Claremont, Hastings.   01424 716481

Old Hastings Preservation Society: All Saints Hall, All Saints Street, Hastings.   01424 421954

The Shipwreck Heritage Centre: Rock-a-Nore Road, Hastings.   01424 437452

Tourist Information Centre: Queens Square, Priory Meadow, Hastings.   01424 781111

INDEX

Numbers in **bold** type refer to illustrations

Abraham's 44, 45

Albert Memorial **64**, 65, 87

Albert, Prince 64

Alexandra Park 65, 72

All Saints Street 12, **14**, **15**, 24

America Ground **58**, 59

Arcoll, Charles 34

Augustinians 60

Baird, John Logie 69

'barking' 8

Barry, James vi

bathing machines **52**, 53

Becket, Thomas à 42

Bird Lady **87**

Black Canons 60

boating lake **37**

boats

    'Albertine' 89

    'Enterprise' 7

    German submarine **93**

    luggers 7, 32

    'Sealink Endeavour' 35

Bourne, The 19, 23, **25**

Bourne Hall, The **23**

Bourne Stream 24, 25

Bourne Street **24**

Bourne Valley 2, 14

Brassey, Thomas 54

Cambridge Road 56, 67

Capel's Restaurant **13**

Capell, Edward 12

Carlisle Parade 52

Castle Street **44**, **45**

Chichester, Bishop of 74

Chichester, Earl of 43

churches

    All Saints 6, **16**, **17**

    Collegiate Church of St. Mary **42**

    St. Andrew's **74**, 75

    St. Mary-in-the-Castle .. **40**, **41**, 43, 97

    St. Nicholas 6

cinemas

    ABC **60**, 61, 69

    Cannon 69

    Classic 69

    Gaiety **68**, 69

Odeon 69

Orion 63

Plaza 63

Public Hall Cinema 63

Ritz 60, 61

Royal Cinema de Luxe 38, 39

Cinque Ports .... vi, 54

Coastguard Station 58

Collier, John 20

Courthouse Street 26

Courts 49

Cricket Ground **72**, 73

Cuckoo Hill 58

De Luxe Leisure Centre **39**

Denmark Place 47, 85

Dickens, Charles 62

Dines, William **83**

'Doom' painting 17

drinking fountain **92**

East Cliff House **12**, 13

East Fort 12

East Hill 2, 14

East Hill lift 11, 13, 26, 90
East Sussex Hospital **56**, 57
East Well **10, 11**, **82**
Edward, Prince of Wales 18, 57
Elizabeth I vi
Elizabeth II 73
English Heritage 41

Figgett's **26**
Fish Street 14
Fishermen's Church **6**
Fishermen's Museum 1, **7**, 97
fishing boats 2, 7
fishing industry vi
Fol-de-Rols 57
F.O.S.M.I.C. 41, 97

General Post Office 67
goat cart **86**
Godfrey, Phyllis 71
Great Bourne Street 22
Gun Garden 43
gun platform 12

Hæstingas vi
Halifax plc **67**
harbour .... vi, 2, 36, 37, 58,72
harbour arm **36, 37**

Harbour Company 36
Harold Place 46, 87, 89, 93
Harold Road **18, 19**
Hastings Castle 3, **42, 43**
Hastings Corporation 32, 43, 51, 55
Hastings Council ... 5, 14, 64, 65, 86, 97
Hastings Museum .... v, 1, 75, 96, 97
Hastings Observer 44
Hastings Pier 3, **54, 55**, 56, 86, 88
Hastings Sports Centre 51
Hastings Station 76
Hastleons 68
High Street 20, 24, 26, 28, 30, 32, **95**
Holy Trinity Priory 60, 61
hotels
    Castle **70**, 71
    Palace 48
    Queens **46, 47**, 53, 86, 89
    Seaside and Pier 48
    Swan **30**, 31

ice house 32
ice-cream seller **85**

James Rock and Son 48
Judges' Photo Store 49
Kay, Joseph 40
Kents 10

Leyland buses **95**
Lifeboat House **34**, 35
Little, Sidney vii
Lloyd, Marie 38
London Trader, The 83
'lute' stern 80

map, Hastings **1**
Marine Parade 34
Market Cross **18**, 19
Market Street 28
Marriott's Photo Stores .... iv, 49
Mastin's **44, 45**
Meadow Cottages **66**, 67
Meadow Road 66
Milnes Daimler bus 74

net shops **4, 5**, 10, 79
Norman Conquest 42

O.H.P.S. 7, 21, 97
Old London Road 18, 19
Old Stables **20, 21**
Old Town .... v, 2, 3, 18, 19,
     23, 24, 25, 30, 32, 33, 35, 37
Old Town 'parade' 47
Old Town Hall **28**, 29
Old Town Museum 1, **29**

Ore Lane 76

Pelham Crescent **40, 41**, 43
Pelham family 43
Pier *see* Hastings Pier
Post Office 64
Priory Farm 60
Priory Meadow Shopping Centre . **73**
Priory Meadows 58, 72
Priory Valley 70, 76
Public Hall **62**
Public Library 1, 29, 97

Queens Arcade 69
Queens Road
        28, 45, 64, 66, 68, 72, 74, 76

Ransom, William 76
Reverend Tom 6
Robertson, Patrick F. 59
Robertson Street 59
Robertson Terrace 86
Rock-a-Nore 3, 6, 10, 36, 37
Rock-a-Nore Garage **9**
Rock-a-Nore Road 8, 32
Rotunda, The **32**, 33

Safeway's 75

Sainsbury's 61
Shipwreck Heritage Centre 1
St. Andrew's Archway **76, 77**
St. Leonards .... vii, 3, 19, 46
St. Mary-in-the-Castle ... **40, 41**, 43, 97
St. Mary-in-the-Castle, Friends of
    see F.O.S.M.I.C.
Stables Trust 21
Stade, The 35
Stone Corner **27**
Swaine, Joseph 17
Swan House **31**

tan house **8**, 9
'tanfrocks' 8
theatres
        Bourne **22**
        Empire Theatre of Varieties **38**
        Gaiety **68**
        Marine Theatre of Varieties 38
        Stables **21**
thresher shark **91**
Tourist Information Centre 1, 97
town centre **63, 65**
Town Hall 28, 29
trams 18, 94
Tressell, Robert 74, 75
Trinity Street 59

Twinkle 57

Victoria, Queen 66
Vine Farm estate 66

Wards 67
Wellington Square **70**
Wellington, Duke of 20
Wesleyans 23
West Hill 3, 14, 42
White Rock vii
White Rock (road) **49, 51**
White Rock Baths **50**, 51
White Rock Brewery 48
White Rock Pavilion 57
White Rock Place **48**, 53
White Rock Theatre **57**
Wilderness, The 25
William the Conqueror .... vi, 42
Woods, George 78, 79, 82, 96